overcoming
backache

TYPHOON
MEDIA CORPORATION

NOTE

This publication is intended to provide reference
information for the reader on the covered subject. It is not
intended to replace personalized medical diagnosis,
counseling, and treatment from a doctor or other healthcare
professional.
**Before taking any form of treatment you should always
consult your physician or medical practitioner.**
The publisher and authors disclaim any liability, loss,
injury or damage incurred as a consequence, directly
or indirectly, of the use and application of the
contents of this book.

Published by:
TYPHOON MEDIA CORPORATION

Overcoming Backache
© TYPHOON MEDIA CORPORATION

Publisher
Simon St. John Bailey

Editor-in-chief
Isabel Toyos

Prepress
Precision Prep & Press

Photos
© Typhoon Media Corporation, © Getty Images,
© Jupiter Images, © Planstock, © J. Alonso

Includes index
ISBN 9781582799537
UPC 615269995396

2010 Edition
Printed in USA

overcoming backache

Why does my back ache?

It's estimated that at least 70 percent of people suffer from backaches, either chronic or sporadic back pain. Backache may be caused by a number of factors, which is why it is important that your doctor diagnose your pains for proper treatment.

✚ In many cases back pains are brought on by bad posture, tension or muscle spasms. These symptoms need medical attention and aren't treated by reducing the time you commute, sit or work. They can become chronic problems. In other cases, backaches are caused by physical ailments. The most common ailments causing backaches diagnosed by doctors are the following:

■ **Degenerative disk.** The disks in the spine are like small sponges that rest between each vertebrae and act as shock absorbers. As we age, they lose their "shockabsorbing" characteristics. Degenerative disk disorder is a result of the normal aging process. But it may also occur as a result of a herity, trauma or direct injury to the disk. As the vertebrae shift, pinching and irritation of the nerve root can happen and muscles begin to tighten and spasm.

■ **Herniated disk.** A disk in the lumbar area becomes herniated when the gel within the disk balloons outward pressing on the nerves around the backbone, producing intense pain.

■ **Referred pain.** Any structure in the lumbar spine can refer pain to other areas of the body. This occurs because the affected part of the spine shares the same nerve supply as the area that the pain is referred to. It's possible that you have a back ailment and pain appears in your arms or shoulders.

■ **Osteoporosis.** Progressive thinning of bone structure with loss of bone calcium, leading to an increased risk of fractures. The spine becomes more compressed, causing posture changes and pain.

■ **Kyphosis (kyphoscoliosis).** Kyphosis refers to a hunching, or forward curvature in the upper part of the spine.

When the degree of kyphosis is above normal then some form of treatment may be required. With aging there is a gradual, and natural, increase in the thoracic kyphosis that gives an appearance of hunching forward more with advancing age.

■ **Scoliosis.** May result from a birth condition developed later in life, most. It usually develops in the upper or in the thoracolumbar area of the spine. The curvature of the spine from scoliosis may develop as a single curve or as an "s".

■ **Lordosis.** Refers to the inward curve of the lumbar spine (just above the buttocks). A small degree of both kyphotic and lordotic curvature is normal, but can get worse with bad posture or excess weight. Lordosis can lead to lumbago or an increased wearing down of the vertebrae.

As with any other ailment, as soon as symptoms appear one should consult a medical practitioner, because for each case there's a treatment that should be followed under the doctor's supervision.

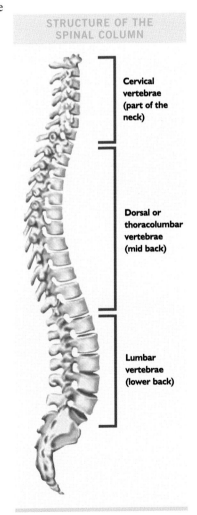

STRUCTURE OF THE
SPINAL COLUMN

Cervical
vertebrae
(part of the
neck)

Dorsal or
thoracolumbar
vertebrae
(mid back)

Lumbar
vertebrae
(lower back)

Preventing and relieving backaches

To prevent or relieve backaches there are a number of healthy lifestyle habits and safe postures you can keep in mind to keep your spine healthy and pain free. It is also advised to exercise regularly to avoid backaches.

There are a number of tips that you can sue to prevent backaches:

■ **Sleeping well.** It's best to sleep in a horizontal position, so that the vertebrae in your spine can readjust, re-hydrate and your back muscles can relax. Back specialists advise using a firm mattress and a solid, low pillow.

■ **Morning stretches.** Beginning your day with morning stretches may be a useful technique in preventing back pain. Before getting out of bed, stretch your arms out over your head as if you were waking up. Next, bring your knees to your chest, one at a time.

When you feel as if your body is ready to get out of bed, roll over to the edge of the bed and use your arm to support your body to get out of bed. With your feet on the floor, put your hands on the bed, on both sides of the body and get up slowly.

■ **Keep a moderate exercise routine.** Exercising regularly, swimming, biking or walking are all great exercises that help your back to stay healthy. Practicing yoga is also indicated for fighting aches and pains, but always under medical supervision.

■ **Lift up your feet.** To relieve mid back pains, a quick relief is to lie in bed and bring your feet to the wall, with your legs at a 90 degree angle with your chest.

■ **Use comfortable clothes.** Tight pants or skirts restrict the body's movements, especially in the waist and back region. You may not be moving properly, causing pain. Fashion should never come before your health.

■ **Fight against osteoporosis.** To prevent this disease, doctors advise eating the daily recommended allowance of calcium, found in many foods and to continue with a regular, moderate exercise routine.

■ **Avoid high heels.** Using shoes with a heel higher than $1^1/2$ in/ 3 to 4 cm is not healthy. High heels force your weight-forward putting extra pressure on your back.

■ **Change your position.** If your work demands that you spend a number of hours sitting, you should get up and walk around each hour. If you must stand on your feet for long periods of time, its best to sit down to do a few tasks.

TAKE CARE WHEN LIFTING HEAVY ITEMS

To lift heavy objects without injuring your back, bend your knees, keep the object in line with your body and never lift the object higher than your waist. Don't trust your sight to let you know how heavy the object is; you should test the weight by lifting it up slightly. If it's heavy, ask for help. Over exerting the back when lifting heavy objects causes most back injuries. If you have to carry a lot of bags when shopping, balance the weight in both arms. If you have to lift heavy luggage, stretch out before carrying the bags: bend over and wrap your arms around your legs.

Correct way to lift objects   **Incorrect way to lift objects**

Correcting your posture with exercises

Keeping a good posture is the first step to preventing back pain. However, if backaches do appear, there are simple ways to help you relieve them.

 A healthy posture, when you're on your feet or walking, is essential for taking care of the spinal column (see *Correct Posture* box). If you feel as if you can't easily change your position, you may need physical therapy to correct your posture.

BEFORE EXPERIENCING INTENSE PAIN

Those who suffer from occasional back pain tend to complain that their pain begins as a slight ache and gradually becomes more intense, something like a sensation of a slight electrical current running through the affected area. Noticing the pain early on can be very useful, because you can use certain methods to lessen the pain or to avoid it. When you sense symptoms it's useful to practice the following tips:

■ **Stretch out.** When your pain begins, it's good to lie on the floor, facing the ceiling and place your feet on a chair or bed, so that your knees and heels are at the same height, at a 90 degree angle in relation to your chest. This posture helps to relieve muscle spasm and lessens the pressure on your vertebrae disks and joints. You should stay in this position for at least 15 minutes.

■ **Lie down in bed.** If you are fighting the initial signs of back pain and the previous position doesn't help, its best to lie down in bed on your back, with your legs straight and a pillow under your knees. Aspirin (acetyl-salicylic acid) or other mild pain medication can help, always under the supervision of your doctor. If you have painful or inflamed muscles, you can use an heating pad.
If the pain gets to be intense, you should take a stronger pain reliever, always following a medical prescription.
If the pain is very severe, it may be best to stay in bed, resting for a few days until the pain subsides.

SITTING DOWN

If you must sit for long periods of time working it is recommended that you use a correct posture:

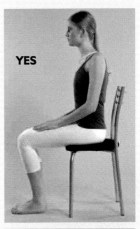

YES

NO

CORRECT POSTURE

Keeping your head in line with your torso.

Shoulders open and relaxed.

Keeping your abdomen and buttocks toned, so that your lumbar spine doesn't curve.

Keeping your feet parallel and about five centimeters apart. When standing, your weight should be distributed equally between both legs.

Exercising the back

These exercises relieve, prevent and stretch out the back. They are very simple routines that you can do at home to prevent and fight against back pain.

FOR CORRECT POSTURE

■ **Exercise 1**

1. With your feet parallel and your knees slightly bent, take a rod in both hands behind your back and hold it with your arms relaxed.

2. Inhale while you stretch your arms backward, feeling how your back curves. Keep your abdomen tight and use your arms for resistance. Release and relax as you exhale.

■ **Exercise 2**

1. Lie with your back firmly against the floor, knees bent, feet parallel on the ground and your arms stretched out to your sides, forming a cross.

2. Close your fists, and raise your arms up keeping your fists parallel above your shoulders. Stay in this position for a few seconds and then return your arms to the initial position. Repeat six times.

STRETCHING

Lie on your back on the ground or on a padded mat. Keep your knees bent; your feet on the ground, in line with your knees, and your arms extended to the sides of your torso. You should note that there is a gap between your spine and the ground. Straighten your torso and stretch it, bringing your whole back firmly to the ground. Feel as if you are pushing your navel downward; contract your pelvic muscles and try to squeeze your buttocks together. Stay in this position for 6 seconds, relax. Repeat 6 times.

EXERCISES WITH A BALL

Before going to bed, take a few minutes to stretch out your back. Place a pillow under your lower back and relax your body for a few seconds. You can also rest your back on an inflated ball of the type used in gyms, which offers a fun and pleasant exercise option.

ARCH

I. *Kneel with your hands and your knees on the ground. Your knees should be hip width apart and your hands should be shoulder width apart. Arch your back, bringing your waist and belly downward toward the ground. At the same time lift up your head and coccyx toward the ceiling. Do this movement slowly and stay in this final arched position for six seconds. If at any moment you experience pain, don't push yourself: stop and relax your body.*

2. Lift up your back trying to curve it as much as you can, while you bring your head down. Stay in this position for six seconds and relax. Repeat six times.

STRENGTHENING YOUR NECK

The three following exercises are based on isometric principles, physical exercises in which muscles act against each other.

1. Wrap your hands around the back of your head, at the base of the neck. Press forward with your hands. At the same time, resist, pressing back with your head. You will feel the muscles in your neck stretch out. Stay in this position for six seconds. Relax and repeat the exercise six times.

2. Place the palm of your left hand over your left ear. Press your head against your hand and at the same time resist, using force with your hand. The pressure should be gentle and constant. Count up to six, relax and repeat six times. Next, repeat on your right side.

3. Intertwine your fingers and place your hands on your forehead. Apply pressure against your forehead with your hands, while you press your head forward into your hands. Count up to six, relax and repeat six times.

EXERCISES FOR SORE BACKS

1. Stand with your knees bent and your feet shoulders width apart, place your hands on your legs, right above your knees, and straighten your back. Arch your lower back and look forward.

2. Inhale and when you exhale bring your left shoulder forward. Keep your elbows firm and look over your right shoulder. Take note of the spiralling motion in the middle back. Inhale deeply, return to the initial position and then lift your right shoulder forward while you exhale. Repeat three or four times on each side.

ROTATING THE SPINE

1. Lie on your back, with your legs bent and your feet pressed to the floor. Make sure that your back is firmly against the floor; use your pelvic muscles to help your back press against the floor.

2. Slowly rotate your knees to the right and then to the left, as if you wanted to touch the floor with your knees. Keep your dorsal spine and shoulders pressed against the floor during the exercise. Repeat six times on each side.

STRETCHING YOUR ARMS AND TORSO

1. Place a pillow under your abdomen and keep your buttocks tight during this exercise.

2. Stretch both arms backward, parallel to your body. Lift your head, your shoulders and finally your chest. At the same time lift your legs as much as you can. Repeat six times.

Yoga for a healthy back

For thousands of years, this Asian technique has been used as a way to balance and maintain the health of the spine. Yoga offers simple and effective techniques to tone the back muscles and to increase their flexibility.

TO AVOID INJURIES
When you are doing yoga positions on the floor, it's best to use a padded exercise mat or a thick blanket to avoid direct contact between the floor and your back.

SAFETY
It is not recommended to do yoga if you are suffering from intense pains.

When the entire spinal column is flexible, it is a sign of health and youth. With our on-the-go society and sedentary tendencies, few people enjoy the benefits of a healthy back. Yoga is a technique dating back thousands of years, its philosophical principles are based on creating harmony between body and spirit. Many yoga exercises use movements that include the entire back, stretching the spine entirely, bringing health and well-being to your back and entire body. *Hatha* yoga, the path of physical yoga is the most popular branch of this system in the West and focuses on physical poses or *asanas*. Most of these work the back muscles, helping to prevent lordosis, kyphosis and scoliosis. Yoga may be an effective relief for pain caused by a herniated disk or degenerative disk disorders. However, you should always consult your doctor before practicing yoga. If chronic back pain is caused by tense muscles, the stretches and movements used during asanas may provide a quick relief for symptoms.

GETTING READY

To warm up your body, many yoga masters recommend beginning with a series of movements called the Rocking chair or

Hammock, which are ideal for releasing tension before moving on to other yoga poses.

Rocking chair

This pose is used as a series of movements practiced at the beginning of a yoga session. The *asana* rocks the body, while at the same time increasing your muscle flexibility, releasing tension, energizing and improving the flow of energy in the spinal cord.

1. Sit on the floor, with your chin pressed against your chest. Bend your legs, with your feet pressed against the floor. Place your hands behind your knees, with your thumbs pointed outward. Keep your chin pressed to your chest to prevent back injuries.

2. Lift up your feet, supporting them with your arms and begin to rock back your body.

3. Rock back and forth five or six times, keeping the legs bent to get the body ready. Inhale and take advantage of the rocking motion to stretch out your legs behind your head. If you can, try to touch the floor with the tips of your toes. Exhale and rock forward, without lifting up your chin. Repeat seven or eight times without stopping. This pose is good for loosening and toning your muscles. Next, lie back down for a minute or two to relax your body.

GENTLE EXERCISE
Yoga is a discipline designed to improve your flexibility and harmony. The exercises use gentle movements without straining your body.

When practicing the asanas remember not to strain yourself. There is no need to push yourself too far. Remember to use gentle movements and don't push your body into a pose. Through time and willpower, you will improve your body's health naturally and get in tune with your body. It is important to remember to use your body with moderation, patience and consistency to prevent side effects like sore muscles or tiredness.

BENEFICIAL ASANAS

After the Rocking chair, which is meant to stretch out your body, the following *asanas* are some of the best exercises to prevent back ailments or to relieve back pains.

Cobra pose

The spine receives a powerful backward stretch, the surrounding musculature is strengthened and the abdominal organs are toned up and massaged.

■ **Half cobra**

This pose is recommended for those who can't reach the full cobra pose. It can also be used to help you prepare for the full cobra.

KEY TIPS
• Wait for at least half an hour after meals and before practicing yoga. Try and eat a light snack an hour and a half before exercising. Or eat a moderate meal three hours before yoga.
• After practicing asanas you shouldn't shower immediately. It's best to wait at least half an hour.

Lie face down, with the legs extended and together behind you. The tops of your feet should be stretched and resting on the floor. With your forehead still on the floor, place the palms of your hands and forearms parallel to your shoulders and head, and lift your trunk from the floor, only up to your navel, with your face looking straight forward.
Stay in this position breathing naturally for a few seconds, then return to the beginning and rest.

■ Cobra

1. Lie down with your legs together and your forehead rested on your hands on the floor. Your legs should be straight with the front of your feet resting on the floor. Use your buttocks to help you move into the next position.

2. Move your hands down to your sides, placing your palms either side of your rib cage and lift your shoulders and sternum from the ground, using your arms for support. Keep your head back, stretching your throat out. Exhale, and return to the initial position.

3. Inhaling, come up as before, but this time use your hands to push the whole of your trunk up. Continue up until you are bending from the middle of the spine. Hold for two or three deep breaths, then exhale and come slowly down. Inhaling, raise the trunk as before, but this time continue up and back until you can feel your back bending all the way down from the neck to the base of the spine. Breathe normally. Hold the position for as long as you feel comfortable, then slowly come down and relax.

Half spinal twist

The movement stretches the spine, tones the spinal nerves and ligaments, and prevents neck and lower back pain. It also helps to remove tension in the waist; because it lengthens the lower back muscles and tones the ligaments.

I. Kneel down with your legs together, resting on your heels. Place the palms of your hands on your thighs. Your back should be straight, your chin and forehead relaxed.

2. Keep your hands in the same place and your shoulders relaxed. Then sit to the right of your feet, as illustrated.

3. Lift your left leg over your right, placing the foot against the outside of the right knee. Bring your right heel in close to your buttocks. Keep the spine erect. Stretch your left arm behind your back, twisting your waist to the left (the palm should be faced outward) and wrap your right hand over your left foot.

4. Look over your left shoulder and twist your shoulders and chest toward the left, without lifting your left foot from the ground. Then come back to the beginning position and repeat on the other side.

Seated forward bend

Helps the sciatic nerves, prevents lower back trouble. Increases the spine's flexibility and stimulates blood circulation in the back.

1. Sit with your feet together, toes pointing at the ceiling. Stretch out the legs and release any tension. Keep your back straight with your arms to your sides. Your hands should be pressed to the floor. Your chest and legs should form a right angle.

2. Take in a deep breath through your nose and stretch your arms above your head, lengthening the spine without arching your back.

3. While you exhale lead with your chest and keeping your back straight, bring your torso forward. Continue right down and hold on to whichever part of your legs or feet you can comfortably reach without bending the knees. Breathe naturally and try to bend forward as you exhale. The correct posture should be with your forehead touching your knees. With practice, you can wrap your index fingers around your big toes and bring your elbows down to the floor, or stretch your arms out over your feet, as shown. To release, inhale while you straighten your torso, keeping your arms stretched out over your head. Next, exhale and slowly lower your arms to the side of your body.

Triangle pose

This standing pose helps to straighten your spinal column and tone the spinal nerves.

1. Stand with your feet well apart (about 3-4 feet). Your feet should be parallel and your arms stretched out at shoulder level. Stand firm and keep your knees slightly bent. Stretch the torso upward while you inhale. Point your right foot outward.

2. As you exhale, bend to the right and slightly forward to bypass your ribs. Your left arm should be stretched out above the head. Slide your right hand down your right leg and hold on to the lowest part you can reach. Look out at your left hand. Take several full breaths in this position before releasing it. Repeat, bending to the left.

Half lobster

Increases flexibility in your back, prevents pain in the sciatic nerves and firms your abdominal muscles.

Lie on your belly, with your chin pressed to the floor. Place your forearms under your pelvis, palms faced down below your thighs. Your legs should stay straight, the top of your feet touching the floor. Inhale and lift up your right leg as high as you can without bending your knee. Stay in this position holding your breath for a moment. Exhale and slowly lower your leg. Repeat on the other side.

Lobster

Works the back muscles fully to strengthen the lumbar spine and the abdominal muscles.

Lie on your belly, with your chin pressed to the floor. Place your forearms and hands under your pelvis. Inhale and lift up both legs at the same time. Hold your breath. To do this pose correctly, keep your buttocks tight and use your arms for strength. Stay in this pose for a few seconds, with your chin against the floor. Then release.

The Plow

This pose helps to keep your back lose, to avoid spinal tension, and stretches the sciatic nerve. This pose may also help to combat obesity because it works the thyroid glands.

1. Begin the position lying on your back, with your legs together, arms down by your sides next to your body and palms of your hands pressed to the floor. Bring your chin toward your chest and press your back muscles to the floor. Inhale through your nose and exhale while you lift up both legs, until they are at a 90 degree angle with your torso. Exhale, then inhale and bring your hips off the floor, supporting your back with your hands.

2. Without bending your knees, stretch out your legs by bringing them behind your head, until your toes touch the floor. Your arms should stay forward, with the palms of your hands pressed to the floor. Stay in this position breathing slowly and deeply. Next, inhale through your nose and slowly lower your legs while you exhale. Concentrate on how each segment of your spine presses against the floor as you bring your back down.

The Fish

This pose strengthens the neck, expands the chest muscles and tones the back and abdominal muscles.

1. Sit on your heels, with your back straight, looking forward and your hands on your thighs.

2. Breathing freely, bring your head all the way back, arching your back. Rest your weight on your elbows and palms of your hands.

3. Drop your head back so that the top of your head is on the floor. You should feel how your vertebrae press together and the area around your throat opens. When you are firmly placed in this position, bring your hands to your chest and place the palms of your hands together. Stay in this position for as long as you find comfortable. To come out of the pose, place your elbows on the floor, inhale, bring your chin to your chest and turn your whole body to the right while you exhale.

The Cow face pose

This pose helps to maintain correct posture, increases your back's flexibility and strengthens your shoulder blades.

1. Kneel down with your legs together, resting on your heels. Keep your back straight, shoulders relaxed and look forward. Stretch your left arm with the palm of your hand facing to the right. Bend your arm backward and place the palm of your hand on your back. Bring your other arm behind your back.

2. Wrap your hands around one another, making sure not to arch your back. Close your eyes and breathe deeply. Stay in this position for as long as you feel comfortable. Release from this position. Repeat with your other arm. (If your hands can't reach each other, you can use a towel, cord or ribbon to help you in this pose. Through time and practice you might not need any assistance.)

The Bridge

This is an *asana* for the lower back region, it stretches the spinal column and relieves tensions where we most often store them: in the back.

I. In a lying position, with your arms extended next to your body and your knees bent, feet together, keeping the balls of your feet pressed against the floor and as close to the buttocks as possible.

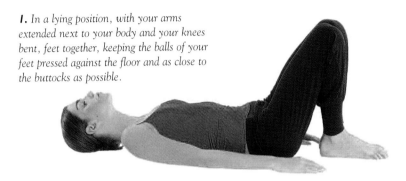

2. *Tighten your buttocks and inhale while keeping your feet pressed to the floor; exhale while you lift up your hips, while keeping your knees pressed together and lifting your bellybutton as high as you can. Stay in this position inhaling and exhaling three times. Each time you exhale try to lift your bellybutton higher. Exhale and lower your body.*

TIP FOR WOMEN

•While you have your menstrual period and during pregnancy, you should avoid yoga poses that put you in a reverse position or those that require a lot of abdominal strength.
•When first beginnig yoga the time that men and women can stay in an *asana* is similar, however progressing over time, women should increase their stamina more slowly and gently than men.
•It's best to practice yoga without makeup, perfumes or lotions applied.

Half wheel pose

This lying pose stretches your neck and back.

1. Lie on your back with your knees bent so that your calves touch your thighs. Your arms should stay at the sides of your body; your hands wrapped around your ankles.

COUNTER-POSE
After completing these postures, it's recommended to do a counter-pose called the Little bear, to massage the lower and mid back. Lying down, bring your knees to your chest and hug them pressing them down on your body.

2. Bring your chin to your chest and lift up your buttocks without moving your hands. Concentrate on your belly button and try to lift it up more with each out breath. Close your buttocks to avoid straining your back. Stay in this position for a few minutes, and release, slowly lowering your body.

The Wheel

Strengthens the back and stretches the neck and the spine.

IMPORTANT

We've put together a guide of yoga poses that might help to keep your back healthy, however, there are safety guidelines that you should keep in mind:

- The Lobster shouldn't be used if you have displaced or herniated disks.
- The Cobra presents side effects for those who suffer from herniated disks.
- Patients who are suffering from serious back trouble shouldn't practice the Plow.

- If you feel pain in your lower back during the Bridge pose you should do the pose with your legs separated and raise the pelvis as high as you can comfortably.
- The Head-to-knee pose should be practiced with care and stay in the pose only if you feel comfortable.
- The Fish pose shouldn't be practiced if you have spinal ailments, dizziness, scoliosis, lordosis or lower back pain.

1. Lie on your back with your knees bent and slightly separated. Your feet should be firmly on the ground. Bend your arms back, with the palms of your hands on the ground right above the shoulders.

2. Bring your chest forward, arching your back as much as you can: flex your buttock and leg muscles to help you. The idea is to distribute the weight of the body so that it's not solely on the arms. Your head should fall back with your neck relaxed. Stay in this position as long as you feel comfortable. Release by bringing your trunk toward the floor, with your chin pressed to the chest and rolling onto your right side to come up.

Head-to-knee
Stretches the back and helps combat lower back pain.

• *Sit with your legs wide apart and your toes pointed to the ceiling. Bend your right leg so that the bottom of your foot rests against your inner right thigh. Inhale and lift your arms above your head. Next, exhale stretching your right leg, trying to wrap your hand around your foot. If you can't reach, take hold of your ankle or shin. Lower each time you exhale. Stay in this position as long as you feel comfortable and release. Repeat on the other side.*

The Camel
Tones the back muscles, especially in the lower back region.

Sit on your ankles. Your back should be straight; your hands on your thighs; you should be looking forward; your jaw relaxed. Lift your body (using your thighs and hips) and slowly bend backward. Place the palms of your hands on the bottom of your feet. You should let your head fall back and lift up your chest forward. Stretch your hips forward as far as you can. Stay in this position, breathing freely and each time you exhale stretching your back a little more, while flexing your buttocks. Release, exhale and relax.

> **COUNTER-POSE**
> After practicing the Camel pose, sit on your heels
> and bring your chest down to your thighs.
> It's important to relax your shoulders; your arms
> should stay at the sides of your body.
> Your head should also drop: the weight will stretch
> out your spine.

MEDITATION CAN ALSO HELP

This practice helps you relax and release the
tension that can cause back pain. This exercise
helps eliminate negative thoughts and calms the
mind to build a connection with the here and
now. It's best to meditate in the Lotus pose,
but because for most beginners the Lotus pose
may be difficult we've included the *Siddhasana*,
which is a simpler pose.

• *Sit on the floor, with your
legs in the form of a V and
your hands placed on your
knees. Bend your right leg,
placing the ball of your foot
against your left inner thigh.
Next, bend your left leg and
place the heel near your
pubic bone.*

• *Close your eyes and pay
attention to physical
sensation, passing
throughout the body
and spinal column,
from the feet to
the crown
of the head.
Inhale and exhale
deeply.*

It's best to stay in this
pose for ten minutes and
allow your thoughts to
pass by without becoming
involved in them.
In this position, your arms
only have one reason:
your physical senses meet
at the palm of your hands.
The practice of meditation
aims to reverse the use of
our senses, not to use
them as we normally do.
The objective is to
eliminate external and
internal interference and
to tap into our vast
sources of pure energy.
At the same time, while
taking deep breaths
internal sounds or *mantras*
("om..." is the best
known) are practiced.
The *mantra* creates a
vibration, which impedes
the flow of thoughts until
they stand still. It's similar
to controlling all
interruptions in your
mind. These are all
techniques, which
allow us to
connect with the
energy of the
Universe.

THE SUN SALUTATION

This is one of the most complete exercises in yoga. The Sun Salutation limbers up the whole body in preparation for the yoga *asana* postures because it uses the spinal column, arms and legs. It helps to prevent backaches, strengthens the sciatic nerves and helps to correct your posture.

2. *Lift your arms above your head and while you are taking a deep breath, separate the elbows, open your hands and arch your spine, with your head back. Exhale.*

3. *Bend your body forward without bending the knees. Relax your neck and touch the floor, your ankles or shins with your hands.*

1. *To begin the Surya Namaskar or Sun Salutation (which is considered one of the most complete yoga exercises) stand on your feet, with your back straight, ankles together and buttocks tight. Bring your hands to your chest with the palms together, take in a deep breath and hold it in for a moment. This gesture has a profound meaning: inner peace (the thumbs together, resting on the body) and peace with the Universe (finger pointed to the sky). Your head and back should stay in line. Inhale and hold in your breath for a moment. Next, exhale.*

4. *In a squatting position, take in a deep breath and extend your left leg back, bending your right knee into your chest. Your right foot should be firmly pressed to the floor. Your hands remain on the floor, below your shoulders to keep your balance.*

5. With your hands on the floor, extend your right leg backward, putting the weight of your legs on your toes, with your ankles together and your arms stretched.

6. Exhale and bend your arms so that your torso touches the ground, keeping your hips elevated for a few seconds. Your body's weight should be distributed to your chin, chest and knees.

7. Inhale and lean on the lower part of your body, while you lift up your chest and shoulders and bend your head backward.

8. Leaning on the palms of your hands, with your feet on the ground, lift your hips up, with your legs extended and your head and neck relaxed.

9. Repeat step 4, this time with your right leg back and your left knee bent into the chest.

10. Repeat step 3: torso lowered, head and neck relaxed, legs extended and hands touching the floor. Stay in this position for a few seconds.

11. Inhale, lift up your body and repeat step 2: head backward, back arched and arms extended upward.

12. Return to the first position, with your back straight and your hands with palms together on your chest. The philosophy of yoga considers that this hand position means peace between body, mind, spirit and Universe.

Relieving shiatsu

Shiatsu is a traditional Japanese technique, thousands of years old, involving finger pressure applied to the feet and palms of the hands to bring the vital *chi* energy into harmony. This ancient therapy might help to prevent illnesses and to relieve pains. It can be done as a do-it-yourself technique, or by a professional *shiatsu* therapist.

IMPORTANT
There are a number of situations in which patients should not be administered *shiatsu*: if you have a fever; if the point is below a mole or birthmark, wart, varicose vein, burn, scar, cut or any other type of skin sore. *Shiatsu* should not be used on pregnant women, especially during the first three months of pregnancy.

In *shiatsu*, presure is applied on some of the body's 354 acupressure points for short periods, as a treatment working on the meridians of the body to put our *chi* or life energy into balance. The technique is based on the principle that physical and mental health are related to the energy that flows through channels or "meridians" along the body, connecting the internal organs to our emotions. Acupressure points are located along these channels. The pressure applied can give effective relief to backaches caused by tension and muscular cramps. As with any other medicine or remedy, especially if you have chronic or intense pains, you should consult a physician to find out if these alternatives are right for you.

PRESSURE POINTS

To sooth back pain there are a number of specific points. These areas can be explored using constant, deep and vigorous pressure, which can be applied with your fingertips or knuckles. When you find the exact pressure point, you may feel a sharp pain, but afterward the pain will go away and you will feel a sense of comfort. The specific points for the back region are as follows:

PAIN RELIEVING POINTS

- For pains in the **lower part of the back**, press on the points mentioned in the boxes B, C, D, F and G.

- If the pain is in the **upper part of the back**, apply pressure to the points mentioned in the boxes A, B, E, H and I.

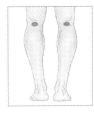

A *Behind the knee, between the two ligaments, in the fold that is formed when the leg is bent. If you have varicose veins here, you shouldn't apply pressure to this point.*

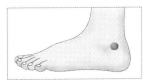

B *Behind the large bone on the outer part of the ankle.*

C *On the point over the external part of the ankle, along the chin bone. In general, pressure is applied combined with the following pressure point.*

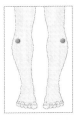

D *The point below the lower part of the knee, between the shin bone and the calve muscle.*

E *Above the collar bones, between the neck and the external part of the shoulders.*

F *In the center of the foot, below the metatarsal arch.*

G *Right below the eyebrow, near the center. To find it you should feel a hollow point along the edge of the eyebrow; the pressure point is just above this point.*

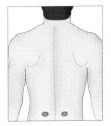

H *On the back, in line with your hipbones, two fingers from the spinal column.*

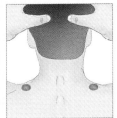

I *Just behind the muscle that runs from the neck to the shoulder, closer to the arm than the neck.*

DO-IT-YOURSELF SHIATSU AGAINST PAIN

The following self-massages are recommended for those who suffer from lower back pain and sciatic nerve problems. The sequences should be repeated twice daily until your pain disappears.

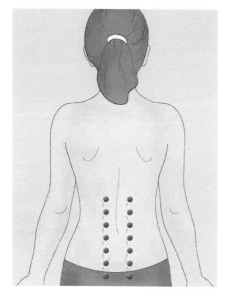

On the waist

Sit down on the edge of a seat, so that you can reach your lower back, the points of the waist that run from the buttocks, tailbone, until the highest part of the back that you can reach with your hands. This sequence ends with the pair of points above the waist. Apply firm pressure simultaneously on both sides.

1. *Place the index, middle and ring fingers of both hands on your buttocks, where your back ends. Apply firm pressure for three seconds.*

2. *Place your hands two fingers higher, following the same line and apply firm pressure.*

3. *Continue climbing up the back, stopping at each point on the back (two fingers higher than the previous point). Firmly press on each point for three seconds. Keep your ring finger, about a finger width away from the spine.*

On the abdomen

The points of the abdomen run vertically in three lines. The first runs down the center; the other two on either side of the center. This exercise can be done lying down or sitting.

1. Place your hands below the edge of your rib cage. Apply moderate pressure for three seconds. Rest.

2. Move your hands in a straight line downward half way between the previous pressure point and the waist. Repeat using moderate pressure.

3. Move down to the point located at the mid point between the waist and pubis. Press two more times for three seconds each time.

4. Place your palms on your abdomen. Apply gentle, simultaneous pressure. Move your hands so that you cover all the points on the abdomen with light pressure. Concentrate on the muscles that seem to be most tense.

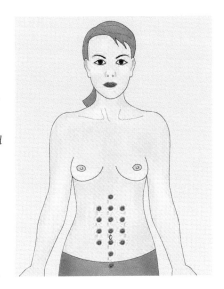

PRESSURE POINTS FOR THE LOWER BACK AND SCIATIC NERVES

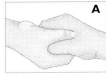

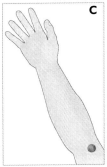

• Use your thumb. Press your hands together, one against the other (A), touching the upper part of the wrist with the index finger. This point lines with your ring finger in a small depression (B). Remember the position of the point; release your hands and apply pressure.

• The point on the inner part of your elbow. Press on this area, finding the point with your thumb.

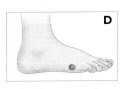

• On the point on the external part of the foot, near the pinkie toe. It is found at the place parallel to where the ball of the foot starts.

• Press your thumb against your index finger. Press the two fingers together so that they form a ring. This is practiced for most problems in the waist region.

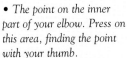

SHIATSU IN PAIRS

This therapy may relieve tensions and blocked energy: it's practiced on the back to relax and reactivate the nervous system. The following pages explain all the secrets to giving a *shiatsu* massage to a loved one.

Initial alignment

1. Sit, crouched over the back of the person receiving the massage. Place the palms of your hands on both sides of the spine.

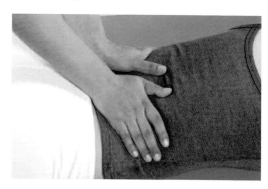

2. Ask the person to inhale, and while he or she exhales, use your weight to apply pressure with your hands over the back and relax the pressure when they inhale again. Rub your hands downward and apply pressure again.

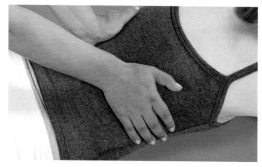

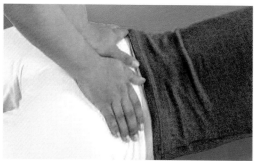

3. Start on the upper back and work downward until you reach the tailbone. Repeat three times.

Balancing the back

Kneel down at right angles in relation to the person receiving the massage. Place your hands in the depression (furthest away from you) that the muscles surrounding the spine form. Rock your partner's body with your hands cupped. You can work down the back at the same time, keeping rhythmic movements. Repeat three times on each side of the back, always placing yourself on the opposite side you are working on.

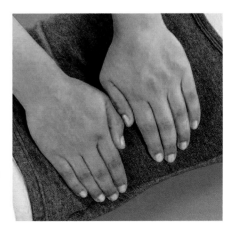

THE SESSIONS

Don't limit yourself to only one session; you should complete several sessions, each lasting an hour. You should see positive results after the first session. It's best to practice **shiatsu** in an ample, well-ventilated and quiet room, with soft music in the background. Massages should be done on the floor or another firm surface.

Cradling the spinal column

This technique centers on the spine itself. Cup the crests of the vertebrae between the thumb and fingers of both hands. Maintaining a firm and continuous contact, move your hands along the whole of the spine, from top to bottom, moving your hands side by side as you go, first one hand, then the other. This loosens the muscles and stimulates the nervous system.

Sawing motion

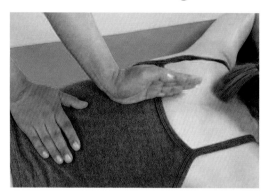

Place your right hand on the lower back of the person who's receiving the massage. Use edge of the palm of your left hand as if it were a knife, making sawing movements on both sides of the spine, moving downward. Apply on one side and then the other side. Repeat three times.

Thumb pressure

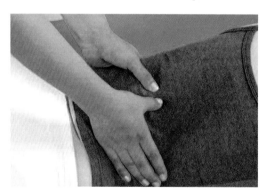

Place your thumbs on both sides of the muscles running along the spine and apply pressure, accompanying the breathing of your partner. Start from the top and work down until you reach the tailbone.

Pressing the tailbone with the palms of your hands

Place one hand above the other on your partner's lower back. Press, concentrating the energy on the base of the spine.

Forearms on the buttocks

I. Sit beside your partner. Separate your partner's legs and apply pressure on the buttocks with your forearm, using a penetrating and rocking action. You should work on both muscles, always working from the side closest to your body and then switching sides.

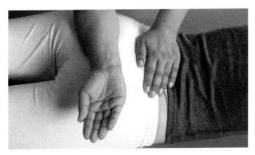

2. *Place the left hand on the lumbar spine and the right forearm on the buttocks. Give the massage by rocking the forearm backward and forward.*

Palm pressure on the legs

You will have to vary your position to reach the entire leg without having to strain yourself. Place your hand on the back of the thigh. With the other, work down the calf pressing with your palm. Repeat on the other side.

THE BENEFITS

This thousand year old technique is very effective to relieve changes in your sleep routine, anxiety, tiredness, depression, stress, over worked nerves and neurosis, all problems that can cause occasional back pains. It also may help to relieve cramps, sports injuries, sprains and it improves your skin tone and brings increased muscular flexibility, mental clarity and concentration. It is beneficial for the joints and helps to correct your posture and improves overall health.

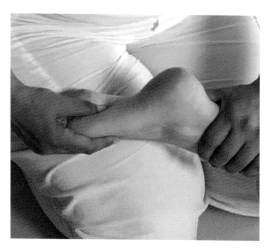

Compressing the foot's surface

Wrap your hand around your partner's ankle and with your other hand apply thumb pressure on the F point (see page 35), a third of the distance between the base of your second toe and the base of the heel. Repeat on the other foot.

Bending the heel to the buttocks

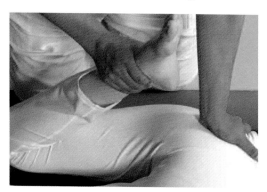

1. Grasp your partner's ankle and bend his leg toward the buttocks. Vary your position to be able to use your weight to bend the leg.

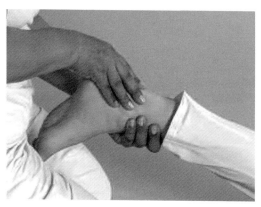

2. Next, position yourself at your partner's feet. Grasp his ankle firmly with both hands and stretch the leg back. Repeat with the other leg.

THE TECHNIQUE

In *shiatsu*, pressure is applied to the points using the palms of the hands, fingers, elbows, forearms, knees and feet, without any instruments or creams. To move the flow of energy, stretches, rotation of joints, rubbing, lifting, rolling and pounding are used.

Bending crossed legs

Cross your partner's ankles and slowly push them toward the buttocks. Do this bend two times, first placing the most flexible leg forward so that it reaches the buttocks and then reversing the legs. Move to the other side of your partner. Without losing contact, change legs and repeat.

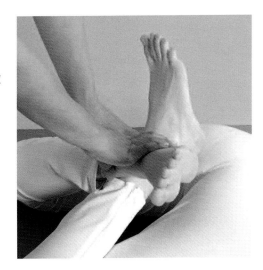

Standing on the balls of the feet

Stand up and stand on the balls of your partner's feet with your heels. Ask your partner to slightly turn the feet toward each other.
Keep your weight on the balls of your feet, not your heels. To complete this exercise, return to the beginning, with the hand on the lower back of your partner. Continue with the contact and then gently interrupt the contact to end the session.

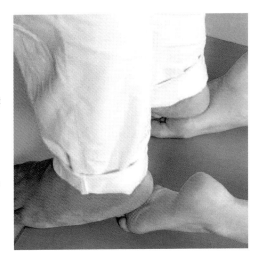

Do-in... for a strong back!

Do-in is an ancient technique related to *shiatsu*
"the physiotherapy of contact." The technique revitalizes and
relieves physical and mental tensions with gentle movements.
These exercises act on the spinal column, stimulating energy flow
and increasing flexibility.

ARMS SWING

1. Stand with your feet shoulder width apart and slightly bend your knees. Let your arms hang to your sides and begin to swing your arms at the height of your hips.

2. Continue swinging your arms, raising them slightly without passing the height of your hips.

3. Let your arms swing higher, so that you feel the spiralling in the center of your back. This motion loosens your thoracic vertebrae and diaphragm. If you swing your arms even higher, to the height of your shoulders, you will loosen the upper part of the spinal column.

THE WAVE

__1.__ Standing with your feet shoulder width apart and your knees slightly bent, place your hands on your thighs, right above your knees and straighten the back. Arch your lumbar spine and look toward the ceiling.

__2.__ Bend your elbows and slowly lower your torso toward the ground, always with your knees bent. Look at the ceiling for as long as you can. Next, let your head fall and curve your back.

__3.__ Contract your abdominal muscles and slowly curve your spine from your tailbone, leaving your head until last. Continue to lift your torso, straightening the spine. Arch the lower back again and repeat this exercise 10 times.

RELAXING POSTURE

When you finish these spinal column exercises, it's recommended to lie on the ground and to relax, with your heels resting on a chair. This way you will relax the lower back and straighten the spine. Close your eyes, breath slowly and feel the energy flowing through your back. Stay in this position for 10 to 15 minutes. You can use this exercise for when you feel pain in this area.

Do-it-yourself express massages

This is a useful guide to simple massages that you can do anywhere and at any time to provide immediate relief for back pains caused by tiredness or daily stress.

1. Sit with your back straight, holding onto your waist with both hands, as seen in the photo. Massage from the inside, outward. Repeat four times.

2. Place the thumbs on the lumbar region and press firmly; if you feel pain, lessen the pressure. Repeat the same sequence on the dorsal or thoracic region.

3. *Apply pressure with your thumbs on the base of the skull where your neck begins. Press and massage your skull with the rest of your fingers, using circular motions.*

4. *Place your hands on your skull. Inhale and while you exhale push your head downward with your hands. You should feel your neck and cervical vertebrae stretching.*

HOW MUCH TIME

You should work on each region between three to five minutes. Once you've finished the massage, it's good to relax your hands and arms because they tend to tense up during the massages.

The body's back bone on the feet

Reflexology is an ancient healing art based on the principle that there are reflexes in the body —especially on the hands and feet— that correspond to the body's organs and glands. Stimulating and applying pressure to the feet or hands can affect the health of other parts of the body, and may relieve back pain.

✚ According to the teaching of reflexology there are points on your feet directly connected to the organs in the body. For example, on the inner edges of both feet there are points that correspond to the spinal column; if you suffer from lower or upper back pain, these pressure points may help to relieve pain in these areas. The reflex points only work when

FOOT REFLEXOLOGY

Press on both feet the areas for the waist, sciatic nerves, tailbone and coccyx. You can also apply pressure to the chest cavity point, to relieve tension. There are also points on the external part of the feet that reflect the sciatic nerves, shoulders and hip. On the internal part of the feet points correspond to the lower back, thorax and cervical areas. And on the top of the feet, points that correspond to the back and shoulder blades.

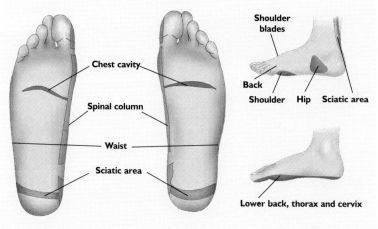

Chest cavity

Spinal column

Waist

Sciatic area

Shoulder blades

Back

Shoulder   Hip   Sciatic area

Lower back, thorax and cervix

there are imbalances in the organs that correspond to the point; the treatment consists of pressing with your thumbs on the point that corresponds to the ailment.

Massaging each point should last about a minute and it's necessary to repeat the massages in a cyclic rhythm, two or three times per session. As with all "physiotherapy of contact" it's necessary to use the treatment regularly: two or three times per week for three to six weeks to get positive results.

MASSAGE TO RECOVER YOUR BACK

1. Start by massaging the entire surface of the foot. Massage the base of the foot with your thumbs, using circular, clock-wise movements to activate and counter clock-wise movements to soften the foot.

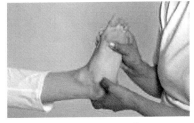

2. Apply finger pressure on the point that corresponds to the spine. Your thumb on the upper part of the foot works the cervical area and the thumb on the lower part, the lower back.

3. With your thumb, apply pressure on the side of the foot, the part that reflects the upper back. With your other thumb, press on the outer part of the ankle to work on the coccyx.

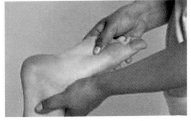

4. Apply pressure on the point that reflects the chest cavity, to balance and harmonize the vital energy in the body. This point is especially important for those who suffer from nervousness or stress.

Nature's soothing power

Natural holistic herb treatments might work as remedies for back aches. Essential oils are used topically to relax, relieve tension and improve the overall health. We've put together a guide of *Essential Oils from A to Z* to know what essentials may work for you.

✚ The following are effective medical plants and herbal remedies used to fight back pains and ailments. Some plants may be easier to find than others depending on where the plants are cultivated. You can find some as fresh plants or dried, and others in liquid form, tinctures, tablets or powder.

Devil's claw
(Harpagophytum procumbens)

- **Parts used.** The secondary storage roots, which form rings when dried. They are used in infusions, to make extracts and mother tinctures.
- Native to Southwestern Africa, the name comes from the curious shape of its fruit.
- Possesses anti-inflammatory and

INFUSION TO FIGHT PAIN

To make the infusion add 3 medium spoonfuls of devil's claw root to 1 cup of water.
Boil for 3 minutes.
Let sit between 10 to 15 hours. You should drink this tincture 3 times a day, 10 minutes before meals.

analgesic properties. Numerous tribes native to Southern Africa have utilized devil's claw for a wide variety of conditions, ranging from gastrointestinal difficulties to arthritic conditions. Devil's claw has been widely used in Europe as a treatment for arthritis.

• **Warning.** Pregnant women should not use this remedy. Since devil's claw promotes stomach acid, anyone with gastric or duodenal ulcers should not use the herb.

AROMATHERAPY

Physical and psychic remedy, using essential oils. Essential oils are extracted from plants, flowers, trees, and roots and processed by grinding, distillation, or extracted with a dissolvent.

Although modern aromatherapy is thought of as a technique to care for the body with pleasant smells, this ancient healing art uses essential oils for their therapeutic properties.

Some uses for essential oils: rub into skin during massages, put a few drops when taking a bath and add to vapors for inhaling. Using oils in massage therapy is the most common use because it awakens the sense of smell, softens the skin and makes the massage feel even more relaxing.

There are a number of essential oils specifically indicated for back pain. Blend and dilute with sweet almond oil or grape seed oil (see Essential oils from A to Z box).

ESSENTIAL OILS FROM A TO Z

BLACK PEPPER

Intense and spicy aroma. This essential oil stimulates circulation, which makes it perfect for relieving pains brought on by exerting physical force.

Safety. It is recommended to use in low doses because it can irritate the skin.

CAMOMILE

There are many varieties, among those made with the common Roman camomile. Because of its soothing and anti-inflammatory properties, it's great for stubborn pains, such as back pain. It blends well with ylang ylang.

Safety. It shouldn't be used during the first four months of pregnancy. In large doses it can have a hypnotic effect and produce drowsiness, although it is not a depressant. Combine with bergamot, geranium, jasmine, lavender and ylang ylang.

WARNING

Essential oils are for external use **only**, they should **never** be ingested. Keep stored away from children and keep away from your eyes.

Lavender
(*Lavandula officinalis*)

• **Parts used.** Flowers and leaves, and sometimes the stems are used to prepare infusions or to make essential oils and tinctures.

• Native to Europe and North Africa. Today, it's cultivated in a number of countries, such as France and the US. In addition, it leaves a lovely, floral scent. The leaves can be added to salads, to substitute for mint.

• Today, lavender is used against headaches, depression and insomnia. This plant has calming and relaxing properties. It can be used as an essential oil for baths or the herb can be used to make decoctions.

SOOTHING LAVENDER TEA

Place 2 teaspoons of lavender leaves in 1 cup of boiling water. Let it steep for 15 minutes. You can drink up to 3 cups per day.

Passion Flower
(*Passiflora coerulea*)

• **Parts used**. The flowers and leaves are used in infusions. The fruit is edible.

• *Passiflora coerulea* originated in the Americas. A species with similar characteristics, is grown in Europe. The plant was brought to Europe by the Spanish conquistadors, who saw in the flower the marks of the passion of Christ (hence the name).

• One of the best remedies against nervous ailments, it doesn't have any side effects. Passion flower has sedative and soothing properties, but not depressive. It also makes you sleepy. Ideal for work related stress and mood swings and nervousness brought on by premenstrual syndrome and menopause.

• **Warning.** Do not use passion flower if you are pregnant or breast-feeding. Do not administer to children under age of 3 years old. For children between 4 and 12 years of age, consult a medical specialist, because the dose should be proportioned to weight of the child. Eat passion fruit only when very ripe, because the fruit has toxic properties before ripening.

ESSENTIAL OILS FROM A TO Z

CINNAMON

This warming oil has invigorating properties, especially recommended for muscular pain. Blends well with citrus essential oils like orange.

Safety. You should always purchase cinnamon oil made from cinnamon tree leaves, because cinnamon bark can irritate the skin. Essential oils made from the leaves should be used in low doses.

GRAPEFRUIT

It is useful in fighting fatigue, because of its stimulating and revitalizing properties. Sweet and citrus aroma, blends well with camomile, lavender and orange.

Safety. It should be used in low dilutions. Avoid direct sunlight after using this oil.

Cayenne Pepper
(*Capsicum frutescens*)

- **Parts used**. The leaves and fruit are used in tincture and powders.
- There are at least 40 species of capsicum native to Central and South America. The fruit is a cylindrical strip of red or yellow color when ripe. The taste is very hot and spicy. It has been used since pre-Hispanic times as a food, medicine and ceremonial ingredient.
- Among its many properties, it's a pain reliever, anti-inflammatory, and antiseptic. It is recommended for swelling, bruising, rheumatism and herpes.

White willow
(*Salix alba*)

- **Parts used.** The leaves, roots and the bark are used and cultivated in the spring.
- It grows in central and continental Europe, although it's also found in North America. Grows in the wild along rivers, streams, forests and in other humid environments.
- Among its active components, salicin is the most important for its pain relieving, sedative, anti-rheumatic and anti-fever properties.

RELIEVING TINCTURE

To take advantage of the pain relieving properties of cayenne pepper, you should let a whole pepper, fruit and seeds ferment in alcohol for 5 hours. Then apply this relieving liquid to the affected area. Avoid touching your eyes, mouth or genitals. Pepper irritates open wounds.

ANTI-STIFFNESS EXTRACT

White willow extract can be found in specialized stores. The dose for average adults is between 60 and 120 mg a day.

• **Warning.** People who are allergic to aspirin (acetyl-salicylic acid) or other similar medicines should not use white willow. It shouldn't be used on pregnant women or children.

European Meadowsweet
Filipendula ulmaria)

• **Parts used.** The flowers and the leaves are sometimes used in decoctions.

ESSENTIAL OILS FROM A TO Z

LAVENDER

This is one of the most versatile and widely used oils. Its pain relieving properties are recommended for muscular pain. It also helps to balance the emotions, because it allows you to release tension. Its clean and floral aroma has sedative effects.
Safety. Do not use this oil during the first three months of pregnancy.

MARJORAM

Has pain relieving properties and increases local circulation.
The aroma is intense and almond like.
Safety. Shouldn't be used during pregnancy.

• It grows in humid areas throughout Europe, except in the Mediterranean. It also grows in some of the northern, cold areas of North America.

• Anti-inflammatory, pain relieving and fever fighting, it can be used against back aches, neck pains and other ailments such as sciatica rheumatoid arthritis, neuralgia and other problems caused by uric arthritis or gout.

RELIEVING COMPRESSES

Prepare a decoction or strong infusion with 3 tablespoons of European meadowsweet in 4 cups of water and apply on the sore areas.

Cat's claw
(*Uncaria tomentosa*)

• **Parts used.** The bark of the roots is used in infusions, tinctures or dried extract.

• It grows in the tropical, mountainous Andes region in South America, especially Peru.

• It has anti-inflammatory and antioxidant properties and is recommended for inflammations, arthritis, rheumatism, and tumors. It is also considered a healing agent.

• **Warning.** It should be used with precaution during pregnancy.

Valerian
(Valeriana officinalis)

- **Parts used.** The roots are used in extracts and tinctures.
- It grows wild all over Europe and in most cases valerian is cultivated to make medical extracts.
- It's a sedative, which is why it is indicated to relieve tense muscles and neck pain, and upper back pain caused by stress.
- It doesn't present any side effects.

ESSENTIAL OILS FROM A TO Z

ORANGE

Sweet, fruit aroma, it's one of the most relaxing citrus oils. Comforting and stimulating, relieves muscular pains and is very useful in baths during the winter.
Safety. You should use it in low doses because it can irritate the skin.

ROSEMARY

Especially recommended for intense pain. It is an intense oil with a clean, herbal aroma. It can help to stimulate your energy when you're energy level is low. It is also an astringent, and contributes to tightening of the skin and pores. It blends well with basil, bergamot, myrrh, and lavender.
Safety. Shouldn't be used during pregnancy.
If you suffer from epilepsy or high blood pressure, avoid this oil.

Diet for a strong back

To prevent and fight backaches it's important to include the necessary nutrients in your daily diet. Many minerals and vitamins not only ensure your overall health, but may help to prevent back trouble.

➕ Although backaches are caused by many factors, it's important that you eat a healthy, balanced diet. On the other hand, keeping correct posture, losing excess weight and building up your muscle mass are other preventative lifestyle habits you should incorporate, because they improve your over all health. Nutritionally, there are a number of different foods you can eat that carry essential vitamins and minerals to keep your back and spinal column healthy. If you eat a diet low in calcium and protein with very few fresh vegetables and instead eat refined carbohydrates, it's important that you change your eating habits. To maintain your back's health and your overall health you should adopt a diet rich in fruits and fresh vegetables, avoiding **animal fat, sugar, salt, alcohol, tea** and **coffee**.

NOTE
You should always consult your doctor before changing your diet.

ANTIOXIDANTS

Sweet potatoes, garlic, oranges, tomatoes and berries are foods rich in antioxidants that help to reduce the free radicals that destroy joint cartilage.

VITAMINS AND MINERALS

Symptoms of vitamin and mineral deficiency can include back pain, low blood circulation in your back, neck tension and overall stiffness. To avoid or to stop these side effects, it's important to eat the correct amount of nutrients that we've listed in the following guide.

Vitamin A

Necessary to keep the bones healthy, to maintain mucous linings and skin cells rejuvenated, it's also an important vitamin for the tendons and muscle tissues. It comes from two natural sources: retinal vitamin A comes from animal sources whereas beta-carotene vitamin A comes from plant sources. Beta-carotene is often referred to as provitamin A. Beta-carotene is a powerful antioxidant and immune system booster. When you have a vitamin A deficiency it's more probable that you'll suffer from joint pain, because the bones and tissues have difficulty in regenerating. It is found in **grains, fruit, dried fruits, vegetables, beans, oils, meats** and **fish**.

HEALTHY BEANS

For your body to correctly digest beans they should be cooked well until very tender. They can be accompanied by vegetables and spices such as carrots, leeks, onion, bay leaf, cardamom, garlic and coriander leaf. You should avoid eating beans with bread and/or animal derived fats. It's most recommended preparing beans with brown rice or whole pastas.

ALGAE SAUCE
Soak 2 tablespoonfuls of hiziki seaweed for 15 minutes. Drain and save the water. Rinse the seaweed. Marinate with 2 medium sized grated carrots, 3 teaspoons of sesame oil for 10 minutes. Add 2 tablespoonfuls of soy sauce, and blend in a blender until it has the consistency of a sauce. Add the necessary amount of the water used to soak the seaweed. This sauce can be used to accompany grains (rice, millet) or spaghetti.

VEGETARIAN ALTERNATIVES

Dried fruits and nuts are very rich in calcium and can be used to substitute milk for people who are lactose intolerant or on a vegan diet. Eating dried fruits and nuts is a great way to maintain healthy bones and to prevent osteoporosis. For children, eating dried fruits and nuts can help to reinforce bones and to accompany proper growth. Some calcium rich options include almonds (240 mg for each $3^1/2$ oz/100 g), hazelnuts (140 mg for each $3^1/2$ oz/100 g) and pistachios (110 mg for each $3^1/2$ oz/100 g).

Vitamin B$_6$

Vitamin B$_6$, also known as pyridoxine, is part of the B group vitamins, is water-soluble and is required for both mental and physical health. It is an important vitamin for the immune system. It supports metabolism, especially proteins. It helps to balance hormones and breaks down fats and carbohydrates. It helps to prevent stress and muscular cramps, which is why it is good to prevent backaches. It helps to prevent extreme tiredness and muscular cramps. It is found in **sunflower seeds**, **dried fruits**, **bananas**, **soy beans**, **nuts** among other **foods**.

Vitamin B$_{12}$

Known as cyanocobalamin, cobolamin and also known as the energy vitamin.

Cobolamin is needed in the manufacture and the maintenance of red blood cells and it stimulates appetite, promotes growth and releases energy.

Found in meat-derived foods and some vegetables. **Meat, chicken, fish, eggs, dairy products, seaweed, mushrooms,** and **brewer's yeast**.

Vitamin C

Vitamin C also known as ascorbic acid together with vitamin E and betacarotene (derived from vitamin A) make up the trio of antioxidants. It's necessary for the production of collagen, which is important for growth and to repair cells in the tissues, blood vessels and bones, it also helps to prevent premature aging. Vitamin C is water-soluble, and is flushed from the body a short time after ingestion, which is why you should consume vitamin C several times a day. Vitamin C is more effective when combined with the active properties found in bioflavonoids (which the white skin in citrus fruit contains), calcium and magnesium. This vitamin is found in fruits and vegetables and it is recommended to eat fresh foods containing vitamin C, before meals or at breakfast. Vitamin C rich foods include **citrus, strawberries, kiwi, guavas, currants, oranges, tomatoes** and **raw red peppers**.

BENEFICIAL FATS

When your back pain is caused by joint ailments, it's recommended eating avocado and soy. Both foods, as with extra virgin olive oil, have properties that are destroyed by heat. They are especially good for joint ailments.

Vitamin D

This vitamin ensures the correct absorption of calcium and phosphorus necessary to keep your bones, joints and nervous system healthy. It's a vital nutrient for the prevention and treatment of osteoporosis. Vitamin D is also referred to as calciferol and can rightly be called "the sunshine vitamin", since the body, in a sunny climate can manufacture this nutrient from the sun shining on the skin due to the presence of colecaciferol or provitamin D_3. Vitamin D can be found in **eggs, butter, liver, cod liver oil** and **whole milk**.

Vitamin E

It is also called "alpha tocopherol", this vitamin is fat-soluble. Vitamin E is a powerful antioxidant, protecting your cells from oxidation, and neutralizing unstable free radicals, which can cause damage. This is done by the vitamin E giving up one of its electrons to the electron deficient free radical, making it more stable. It helps to relieve fatigue and contributes to muscular and skeletal health. It is found in **raw vegetable oil**, **dried fruits**, **avocado** and **wheat germ**.

Calcium

Calcium is needed for so many different functions in the body, from bones to

OMEGA-3 FATTY-ACIDS

Ocean fish (salmon, sardines, codfish, and tuna) are rich sources of Omega-3-fatty acids, an important component for fighting arthritis. As an alternative to fish, you can use flaxseed or flaxseed oil.

BROTH TO SOOTH JOINT PAIN
Boil thoroughly washed peeled skin of
3 or 4 potatoes, and drink this broth
as if it were a soup, 2 times a day. It's a
wonderful source of minerals.

blood clotting and function of muscles.
Calcium rich foods include **milk**, **cheese**,
yogurt, **leafy green vegetables**, **sardines**,
wholegrain cereals, and **calcium enriched
soymilk**.

Magnesium

Magnesium helps with formation of bones
and teeth and assists the absorption of
calcium and potassium. Where calcium
stimulates the muscles, magnesium is used
to relax the muscles. It is used for the
muscle tone of the heart and assists in
controlling blood pressure. Vital for the
cellular function that helps the body to
produce energy. Magnesium deficiency is
related to other nutritional deficiencies,
brought on by poor diets made up of frozen
or processed foods. Found in **green
vegetables**, **bananas**, **wheat germ**, **fish**,
seaweed and **dried fruits**.

Potassium

Potassium is one of the electrolytes we all
require to maintain health. It is needed for
growth, building muscles and transmission
of nerve impulses. It's a fundamental
mineral to keep the back healthy and
muscles strong. Can be found in **fruit** and
garden vegetables, especially **potatoes**,
cauliflower, **tomatoes**, **bananas**; it is also
found in **salmon**, **pork** and other foods.

FOODS YOU SHOULD AVOID

**When you are suffering
from back problems it's
best to avoid eating:**

• **Wholewheat grains**,
contain phytate, which prevents
absorption of calcium, creating a
deficiency of calcium in the
body, putting the health of the
bones at risk.

• **Acidic foods and drinks**
that can provoke gastritis or
gastric acid. The body, in order
to compensate for excess acid,
tends to use calcium from the
bones to balance the pH acid in
the stomach to make it more
alkaline. It's best to avoid
drinking: coffee, tea, cola drinks
(all containing caffeine, which is
acidic), alcohol and refined
sugars.

• **Excess dairy products**,
which for some people causes
excess acid. In some cases it
maybe best to include other
foods rich in calcium other than
dairy products.

• **Excess of salty foods** can
also reduce the calcium in the
body, especially for the elderly.

• **Foods rich in oxalates**
(rhubarb, spinach, and beets)
may decrease calcium
absorption and retention,
resulting in lower calcium levels
in the body.

index